Ephesians

The Church,
The Body of Christ

By Craig McCourt

Ephesians: The Church, The Body of Christ

Second Edition including leader's guide ©2022 Craig McCourt

First Edition ©2016 Craig McCourt

Copyright © 2016, 2022 Craig McCourt All rights reserved.

No part of this publication may be reproduced, stored, or transmitted in any form or by any means—for example, electronic, photocopy, or recording—without prior written permission. The only exception is brief quotations in printed reviews. Please encourage and participate in doing the right thing.

Write to: info@godponders.org

All Scripture quotations, unless otherwise indicated, are taken from the Holy Bible, New International Version®, NIV®. Copyright ©1973, 1978, 1984, 2011 by Biblica, Inc.™ Used by permission of Zondervan. All rights reserved worldwide. www.zondervan.com The "NIV" and "New International Version" are trademarks registered in the United States Patent and Trademark Office by Biblica, Inc.™

The Holy Bible, English Standard Version® (ESV®)
Copyright © 2001 by Crossway,
a publishing ministry of Good News Publishers.
All rights reserved. Used by permission of Good News Publishers.

227.507

Interior design by GodPonders Publishing

Cover design by Craig McCourt

Originally released in 2016 by GodPonders Publishing

DEDICATION

To God be the Glory—Great things He has done.

To my bride and partner Shirley, who has journeyed this life with me for more than 36 years as we discover the amazing blessings, strength, hope, and power found within the body of Christ.

I will long remember the example of genuine care and concern shown to me and my family by the body of Christ at Trinity Lutheran Church in Waconia, Minnesota. They reflected the body of Christ when we needed it the most.

TABLE OF CONTENTS

Acknowledgements	1
How to Use this Study Guide	3
Introduction to Paul's Epistles	5
One – (1:1-14) *Election by Grace*	7
Two – (1:15-23) *Prayer for the Church*	15
Three – (2:1-11) *But God...*	19
Four – (2:11-22) *We Are One in the Spirit*	25
Five – (3:1-13) *The Ministry of Grace*	31
Six – (3:14-21) *Prayer for the Disciple*	37
Seven – (4:1-16) *The Church United*	43
Eight – (4:11-32) *A New Way of Thinking*	51
Nine – (5:1-33) *The Marriage Chapter*	57
Ten – (6:1-24) *Armor Up*	65
Bible Study Leader Guide	75
About the Author	85

ACKNOWLEDGEMENTS

I want to thank the many small Bible study groups that have helped to refine this study over the past several years: Cross View Lutheran in Edina, MN; New Creation Lutheran in Shakopee, MN; and St. Michael's Lutheran Church in Bloomington, MN.

Thanks to my wife Shirley McCourt for helping me write the leader's guide portion of this book.

Great thanks to a former youth ministry student and now faithful wife, mother, and fantastic editor Melissa Peitsch.

How to Use this Study Guide

With Your Small Group

This study is a chapter-by-chapter, verse-by-verse study of the Book of Ephesians. The best way to use this book is to distribute copies to the participants of your group in advance of the studies. Encourage them to work through the questions on their own, so that when you come together as a group, each individual can share their personal insights gained. It may also be used effectively as an actual "group study" by working as a group each week through the questions contained in each unit.

Each lesson is designed to be completed in 45-60 minutes. Many of the chapters are divided into two studies. Feel free to use those divisions as simple suggestions, not hard and fast starting and stopping markers. Work with your group to develop a consensus on how much time you want to spend on each study.

Each study contains the invitation to read a portion of Ephesians followed by questions based on that portion of Scripture.

 *PONDER THIS: Throughout the study, you will find the ponder drawings and a Ponder This question for personal reflection. You can discern whether your group members' comfort level allows these questions to be shared with the group or whether they should be used simply for personal reflection.*

Enjoy the study, enjoy the Word, and be blessed as you study. The leader's guide in the back of this book will provide tips for a successful group study and suggest possible answers to the study questions.

Introduction to Paul's Epistles

Ephesians, Philippians, Colossians, and Philemon comprise the Prison or Captivity Epistles, which were so named because Paul was in prison when he wrote them. There are two known imprisonments of Paul. One was in Caesarea under the governorships of Felix and Festus (Acts 23–26) and another in Rome while Paul awaited trial before Caesar (Acts 28). Supported by a small amount of early Church tradition, some scholars have conjectured another imprisonment in Ephesus during Paul's extended ministry there. Paul mentions "frequent" imprisonments in 2 Corinthians 11:23, but these probably refer to overnight stays in jail, as at Philippi (Acts 16:19-40). The traditional view assigns all of the Prison Epistles to Paul's Roman imprisonment.

Introduction to Ephesians

THEME: Ephesians was not written in response to a specific circumstance or controversy, as were most of Paul's epistles. It has almost a meditative quality. In the theme shared with Colossians—Christ the head of the Church, His body—Ephesians emphasizes the Church as Christ's body, whereas Colossians emphasizes the headship of Christ. Colossians warn against false doctrine, which diminishes Christ, while Ephesians expresses praise for the unity and blessings shared by all believers in Christ.

The letter is comprised of two parts. In the first part, Paul paints a picture of what the church is. Paul was the perfect apostle to contemplate what the church is since he spent many years ministering to people, establishing congregations, nurturing, and equipping these congregations. Paul never uses the word denomination in his definition of the church, for these are artificial creations in a broken reflection of God's church. As Paul reminds us, the church was established to include all who placed their trust in God's Son, Jesus Christ, as the only Savior from sin.

In the second part of this book, Paul talks to us as induvial members of the church. He reminds us what it means to be a member of the church of Christ. He encourages us to live bound together in the spirit of unity, reflecting the light of Christ to the word.

AUDIENCE: Was the letter addressed to the church in Ephesus? The earliest manuscripts do not have the words "in Ephesus" in the salutation (1:1). This is noted in the Revised Standard Version. The letter itself nowhere indicates that Paul and the readers whom he is addressing are personally acquainted with one another. There are passages which indicate the very opposite (Eph. 1:15; 3:2). When we consider how long Paul ministered in Ephesus and what close ties that ministry established (Acts 20:36-38), the absence of any personal touches in the letter is very striking. Similarly, the letter gives no hint that Paul is personally acquainted with the life of the church—there are no concrete details, no reminiscences of former personal contact. Paul's letters to the Corinthians, written to a church in which he had worked and with whom he was intimately acquainted, present a striking contrast to the letter to the Ephesians in this respect. One can hardly avoid the conclusion that the letter known as the letter to the Ephesians was not originally addressed to Ephesus, or at least not to Ephesus alone.

ONE

Ephesians 1:1-14
Election by Grace

"In him we were also chosen, having been predestined according to the plan of him who works out everything in conformity with the purpose of his will, in order that we, who were the first to hope in Christ, might be for the praise of his glory."
Ephesians 1:11-12

Outline of Ephesians Chapter 1

1-2	The Salutation (author, addressees, time, place)
3-6	How we become members of the Church (election)
	Redemption through the blood of Christ (our election carried out in time)
8-9	The work of the Holy Spirit (Redemption applied to men)
10	The unity of the Church
11-14	Who belongs to the Church
15-19	Paul's first great prayer for the Church
20-21	The Exaltation of Christ, and power of the Resurrection
22	Christ is the Head of the Church
23	The Church is Christ's Body—Christians are members of His body

Recently, a Capital One Bank commercial contended that the decision to choose their bank was the easiest decision in the history of decisions. They gave an example of an easy decision: former NBA star Charles Barkley was in a lineup of children waiting to be chosen for a game of playground basketball. Charles Barkley was chosen first, to the shock of no one.

I have been in those schoolyard lineups, and I must admit I was never chosen first. I remember a few times when the selection ended with the words, "and you get McCourt." As we begin our study of Ephesians, we see the Father choosing us to be a part of the Church—the body of Christ. But this decision was certainly not as straightforward a call as picking Charles Barkley. Were it not for the grace of God in Christ, we might still be in the lineup. Instead, we will discover the will of God, which chose us in Christ before the foundation of the world.

Read Ephesians 1:1-14

1. Although virtually nothing is stated directly about the people Paul is writing to, what can you infer about them from these first 14 verses of his letter?

2. How does Paul use the word "Apostle" in verse 1 when he talks about himself? (see Acts 26:15-18; 1 Thess. 2:6)

3. What does the word "saint" mean as it is used here? (v. 1)

4. Are you a saint? Is it difficult or easy to consider yourself a saint? Why?

5. What is the significance of the words "from God our Father and the Lord Jesus Christ"? (v. 2)

PONDER THIS: According to verse 2, where does the grace and peace that Paul extends to the church come from? When you extend grace and offer peace to someone do you give credit to God, or do you think yourself the "bigger person" for having been gracious? How might your attitude need to change?

6. Read through verses 4-10 below, and identify the subject of the underlined pronouns. Then mark each pronoun accordingly with F for Father or S for Son.

> [4] For he chose us in him before the creation of the world to be holy and blameless in his sight. In love [5] he predestined us to be adopted as his sons through Jesus Christ, in accordance with his pleasure and will-- [6] to the praise of his glorious grace, which he has freely given us in the One he loves. [7] In him we have redemption through his blood, the forgiveness of sins, in accordance with the riches of God's grace [8] that he lavished on us with all wisdom and understanding. [9] And he made known to us the mystery of his will according to his good pleasure, which he purposed in Christ, [10] to be put into effect when the times will have reached their fulfillment--to bring all things in heaven and on earth together under one head, even Christ.
> **Ephesians 1:4-10**

7. What does this tell us about our salvation?

8. What does this intermingling of pronouns tell us about the work of the Father and the Son?

9. What does it mean to have "redemption"? (v. 7)

While Paul does not use the word "church," this is where he begins to talk about Christ as the head of the Church, and of all things in heaven and on earth. (1:10)

10. Who belongs to the Church? (v. 11-14)

11. Verse 13 speaks of a seal. What is this seal? How did you receive the seal?

The power of the Spirit in us is a down payment (assurance) of the glory to come. The Greek word for "deposit" is the modern word in Greek for wedding/engagement ring. An engagement ring is a great symbol between a man and a woman, as baptism is between Christ (the groom) and His bride (the Church). Baptism is a sign and pledge of the wedding day between Christ and His Church which is yet to come.

Fun fact: This week we looked at the longest sentence in the Bible (v. 3-14, which tells us the full story of salvation). Next week, we will look at the second longest sentence of the Bible (v. 15-23). Paul surely could have used a grammar lesson on the headache of run-on sentences....

Prayer

Jesus, stir up your strong Spirit to guide us as we ponder what it means for us to be chosen by you. Remind us of your amazing grace given to us, help us live out our adoption as your children, and allow us to give you praise for our great inheritance. Be with us as we continue a study of your Word and let your living and active work speak into our lives. Amen.

For Next Week

As you prepare for next week, read through the entire book of Ephesians. Then make a list of reasons to be thankful for your local church, the body of Christ. Also, consider what verse from chapter one most stood out and why you think that was.

Memory Challenge

7 In him we have redemption through his blood, the forgiveness of our trespasses, according to the riches of his grace...
Ephesians 1:7

TWO

Ephesians 1:15-23
Prayer for the Church

"For this reason, ever since I heard about your faith in the Lord Jesus and your love for all the saints, I have not stopped giving thanks for you, remembering you in my prayers."
Ephesians 1:15-16

Read Ephesians 1:15-23

1. Sometimes prayer can be like pushing a full wheelbarrow—with no wheel. At other times it's like rushing down the rapids of a mountain river. What makes the difference?

2. When you pray for fellow Christians, how do you usually pray for them? Give some specific examples.

3. In verses 15-16 Paul says, "For this reason... I have not stopped giving thanks for you, remembering you in my prayers." Why is Paul so thankful in his prayer for the Ephesians?

4. Why do you suppose these things were so important to him? (See Matthew 22:37-40)

5. What three things does Paul pray for them to see? (v. 18-19)

The word "exceedingly" in verse 19 translated as "incomparably" (NIV), or "immeasurably" (ESV) which Paul uses to talk about God's power is used only five times in the whole of Scripture—a word with a great deal of power!

It is better to take verse 22 in the sense that God "gave" Christ to be head over all things for His Church. He is not only the head **of** the Church, but He is also the head **for** the Church. He is Lord of His Church all right, but He is also vitally united with it and functions through it. He uses all things in the world for the good of His Church. That Church is described as the "fullness" or complement of Christ, just as the body with the head makes a complete man.

6. How is Ephesians chapter 1 itself an answer to the prayers Paul has been praying for his readers? (see verse 15)

PONDER THIS: *Paul prays for the Ephesians to get to know God better. What kinds of things do you do to get to know someone better? How might this apply to your relationship with Christ?*

PONDER THIS: *When was the last time you prayed to have the eyes of your heart enlightened? Why might you be afraid to pray that prayer for yourself? Read Psalm 139 as you ponder these questions.*

Prayer

Lord, give to us a love for your Church. Help us to see the body of Christ as a living representation of you in this world. Though imperfect, may we strive to live and love as the body of Christ reflecting the beauty of the Lord of the Church, Jesus the Christ.

For Next Week

As you prepare for next week, read Ephesians 1:1–2:10, especially pondering verse 2:10.

Memory Challenge

[22] *And he put all things under his feet and gave him as head over all things to the church,* [23] *which is his body, the fullness of him who fills all in all.*

Ephesians 1:22-23

THREE

Ephesians 2:1-11
But God...

"But God, being rich in mercy, because of the great love with which he loved us, even when we were dead in our trespasses, made us alive together with Christ—by grace you have been saved—"
Ephesians 2:4-5 (ESV)

Outline of Ephesians Chapter 2

1-3	Description of natural man before conversion
4-7	Conversion to Christ by grace alone
8-9	Salvation by grace through faith in Christ
10	Saved to serve
11-13	The Gentiles became members of the Church through the blood of Jesus
14-19	Christ has abolished the Jewish Ceremonial Law—the unity of the Church
20	Christ and His Word are the foundation of the Church

21-22   The nature of the Church: "A holy temple of the Lord"

I spent several years working in retail, discovered that managers can be as different as day and night. Perhaps you have worked under someone who was always critical, pointing out mistakes and disparaging, "Don't you know how to do anything?" I worked for one of those bosses, and when our store changed managers (for the better), the employees went from dreading work to enjoying work. Criticism was replaced with encouragement. Even when we needed correction, it was done with gentleness and not judgment. It was transformational. That is a good name for what we find today in Ephesians: Transformation.

We will look at one of the best-known verses in the book of Ephesians, "By grace you have been saved, through faith" (2:8). This is also one of the cornerstone verses for Lutheran theology. GRACE has often been defined by the acrostic, God's Riches At Christ's Expense. In this chapter, Paul contrasts what we are by nature (dead in sin) to what we are in Christ—made alive!

Read Chapter 2 of Ephesians

1. "You were dead in your transgressions and sin." How does sin kill?

2. How might your life be different if God ceased to be gracious?

3. What motivated God to save us? (v. 4-7)

4. Why are these motives so unbelievable, considering our condition as non-Christians? (v. 1-3)

5. What phrase does Paul repeat in verse 5 from verse 1? Why is that repetition significant?

6. Does verse 10 contradict verses 8-9? Why or why not?

Matthew writes in Chapter 10 verse 8, "*Heal the sick, raise the dead, cleanse those who have leprosy, drive out demons. Freely you have received, freely give.*" Freely you have received (that's justification); freely give (that's sanctification).

Having been saved from sin and death by the life, death, and resurrection of Christ, we are justified—declared righteous. We are clothed in Christ's righteousness in our baptism. Having received such a great gift, we are called by the Spirit to live a life of sanctification.

7. What are the "good works" God prepared for us to do?

 *PONDER THIS: Good works are not necessary for salvation, for we are saved freely by God's grace, but they are necessary in the life of the redeemed. How can this be?*

Prayer

Lord Jesus, bless us to take from your Word today a message of forgiveness and grace as we seek to live life as your workmanship in our world. May our daily life reflect your calling on our lives as we seek to show the world who you are through our actions. Amen.

For Next Week

As you prepare for next week, read through chapter 2 and reflect on your life before Christ and after Christ. Also, note any verses from this passage that stand out to you.

Memory Challenge

[10] *For we are his workmanship, created in Christ Jesus for good works, which God prepared beforehand, that we should walk in them.*
Ephesians 2:10

FOUR

Ephesians 2:11-22
We Are One in the Spirit...

*"In him the whole building is joined together
and rises to become a holy temple in the Lord.
And in him you too are being built together
to become a dwelling in which God lives by his Spirit."*
Ephesians 2:21-22

Many of us have sung, "We are one in the Spirit; we are one in the Lord." But we also continue to find ourselves at odds with other Christians who believe or live differently than we do. Such problems were just as common in Paul's day as in ours, as we will see in chapter two.

Read again verses 11-22.

1. What does Paul want his readers to remember according to verses 11-12?

2. How does verse 11 emphasize the ill feelings between the Jews and Greeks?

3. What name-calling do Christians engage in today—perhaps even using biblical terms?

4. Besides some of the superficial differences between Jews and Gentiles, there were also some very real divisions. What are some of the things that divided Gentile from Jew? (v. 12, 14)

5. What does Paul want his readers to remember in verses 13 and 19?

6. According to verses 14-16, how have Jew and Gentile become one?

As you may recall, the name of this study is *Ephesians—The Body of Christ*. We will look more at what Paul has to say about the Church being one body and everyone being a part of it. But have you ever pondered the fact that through one body—Christ's on the cross—the sin of everybody of every language, every culture, and every tribe were brought together to form one sacrifice.

7. What is the significance of the "one Spirit" as expressed in verses 17-18? (see also 4:3-6)

8. What are the images that Paul uses in verses 19-22 to emphasize the unity Christians have with one another?

9. What is the significance of the statement "built on the foundation of the apostles and the prophets, with Christ Jesus himself as the chief cornerstone..."? (see also Luke 24:27)

 **PONDER THIS:** *I have often heard it said, "You can learn a lot from reading books by dead guys" Why might that be true?*

While many people begin their journey toward Jesus through a reading of the Gospels (and that is a great place to start), they miss the wealth of information about Christ in the Old Testament. Martin Luther held that you can learn more about Christ in the Old Testament than you can in the New Testament. He was in good company. Jesus also begins the telling of His story with the Old Testament. *"And beginning with Moses and all the Prophets, he interpreted to them in all the Scriptures the things concerning himself."* **Luke 24:27 (ESV)**

10. How is the Trinity (Father, Son, and Holy Spirit) expressed in verse 22?

11. What does the chapter tell us about membership in the Holy catholic Church? (catholic with a small "c" represents the universal Christian Church)

 **PONDER THIS:** *Is it natural to respond to a gift by asking, "How much do I owe you for this?" How do you sometimes find yourself responding to God's gift by attempting to pay Him back? What might a better response be?*

Prayer

Awesome God, as we leave this place, we put our trust in you, for your promises are faithful and true. We hope continually in you and praise you more and more each day. May we tell of your righteousness as we leave this place and even when we come back. Be our guide in everything that we do and lead us back to Jesus who is our peace. Help us to abide in your Word and let it guide us in all that we do. In Jesus' name, we believe and pray, Amen.

For Next Week

As you prepare for next week, read through the first three chapters of Ephesians. Consider a verse or two from chapters 1 and 2 that stood out to you on this reading.

Memory Challenge

[13] *But now in Christ Jesus you who once were far off have been brought near by the blood of Christ.*
Ephesians 2:13

FIVE

Ephesians 3:1-13
The Ministry of Grace

"I became a servant of this gospel by the gift of God's grace given me through the working of his power. Although I am less than the least of all God's people, this grace was given me: to preach to the Gentiles the unsearchable riches of Christ,"
Ephesians 3:7-8

Outline of Ephesians Chapter 3

1-8   Paul, an apostle by the grace of God

9-10   The purpose of Paul's ministry

11-15   Christ, the exalted Ruler of the Church

16-19   Paul's second great prayer for the Church

20-21   Doxology and conclusion of Part 1

Prisoner and Preacher

Paul wrote this letter when he was in prison in Rome awaiting trial before Nero. He was waiting for the Jewish prosecutors to come with their bleak faces, their deep hatred and their malicious charges. In prison, Paul had certain privileges—he was allowed to stay in a house which he rented and his friends were allowed access to him. Night and day he was still a prisoner. He was watched at all times by the Roman guard whose duty it was to never let Paul escape.

In these circumstances Paul called himself "a prisoner of Christ." Any ordinary person would have said that he was a prisoner of the Roman government; and so he was. But, Paul never thought of himself as a Roman prisoner, only a prisoner of Christ.

It is all in the point of view. When we are undergoing hardship, unpopularity, or material loss for the sake of Christian principles, we may either regard ourselves as the victims of men or as the champions of Christ. Paul is our example. He regarded himself not as the prisoner of Nero, but as the prisoner of Christ.

What do you think of when you hear the word "church"? A building with a steeple, a vibrant fellowship, or a stuffy group of religious hypocrites? Paul's special ministry enabled him to enlarge our conception of the Church.

1. Think of two or three adjectives which summarize your attitudes and experiences of the Church. Explain.

Read Ephesians 3:1-13

2. What gifts of God's grace does Paul say he has received? (v. 2-3, 7-8)

MYSTERY: *something that has always been, but was hidden from view that has now been revealed through Christ.*

3. What is the mystery of Christ that Paul speaks about in verses 2-6?

Note: The modern translations of Ephesians break verses 6-7 into what seems to be separate paragraphs. However, they are a continuation of thought. The verse divisions were set, at times poorly, without divine inspiration but by man. The phrasing used in the Greek expresses one complete thought. Verse 8 starts a new thought.

4. How are verses 8-13 connected with the mystery given to him?

5. Why was this such a "mystery," especially to Paul?

6. What purpose does God have for the Church? (v. 10-11)

7. How does this mesh with God's overall purpose in Christ described in 1:9-10?

 *PONDER THIS: Paul describes himself in verse 7 in the NIV as a "servant of the gospel." What does it mean for you to be a servant of the gospel today? What can you do to improve your "service" for the Kingdom?*

8. Paul begins this prayer with the words "for this reason..." what is the reason or cause for this prayer?

Prayer

Father, we want to thank you for being with us throughout this study. Your presence has been in this place from the start to the end, and we want to say thank you. Lord, as we leave this place, let us go out there and be the salt and light. May we learn more and more how to bless the Church, and be blessed by the Church. Help us to make a difference in this world for the glory of your name. In Jesus' name we believe and pray, Amen.

For Next Week

As you prepare for next week, read through chapter 3. Pause as you begin verse 14 and take into account verses 1-13 set up the "reason" of verses 14-21.

Memory Challenge

[7] *Of this gospel I was made a minister according to the gift of God's grace, which was given me by the working of his power.*
Ephesians 3:7 (ESV)

SIX

Ephesians 3:14-21
Prayer for the Disciple

"For this reason I bow my knees before the Father"
Ephesians 3:14 (ESV)

Read Ephesians 3:14-21

1. Paul begins his prayer by doing what? What is the reason for his posture?

2. What four things does Paul pray for in verses 15-19?

3. Paul prays for understanding or comprehension in verse 18. What are they to comprehend?

4. Why might this have been difficult for them?

5. How does this prayer differ from the checklist prayers we often pray?

6. What difference would it make in our prayer life if we focused on the "why" of prayer versus the "what" of our prayer?

 *PONDER THIS: Paul talks of a "love that surpasses knowledge." What do you need to do to help your love surpass your knowledge?*

A Doxology for the Church

"Now to him who is able to do immeasurably more than all we ask or imagine, according to his power that is at work within us, to him be glory in the church and in Christ Jesus throughout all generations, for ever and ever! Amen."
Ephesians 3:20-21 (NIV)

This is the only doxology for the Church in all of Scripture. This God who created you can do all things. Note that this glory to God is to be "in the Church." The Church is the avenue of God on earth. Here He works. If you want to know God or worship Him, then this should be done "in the Church." Revelation from God comes within the Church.

7. How does this doxology tie together the main themes that have run through the first three chapters of Ephesians?

8. In these last two verses Paul invites us to pray boldly to our Father. Why?

 *PONDER THIS: Has your conversation in the car on the way home from church ever painted the Church in a bad light? How do you think Christ feels about someone speaking poorly about His Bride? How would you react to someone speaking poorly about your spouse?*

Prayer

Holy Father, how majestic is your name! We give thanks that you are ever mindful of us. We thank you for how you have blessed this study. We have been enriched by these lively discussions where we have been free to express ourselves. We thank you for the fellowship we have enjoyed and how we have been taught by each other. We thank you for broadening our minds through each person sharing their ideas. Keep us in your grace until we meet again. Amen.

For Next Week

As you prepare for next week, read chapters 3 and 4. Note the times that Paul prays for "you" or speaks directly to "you" in these verses.

Memory Challenge

[20] Now to him who is able to do far more abundantly than all that we ask or think, according to the power at work within us, [21] to him be glory in the church and in Christ Jesus throughout all generations, forever and ever. Amen.
Ephesians 3:20-21 (ESV)

SEVEN

Ephesians 4:1-16
The Church United

*"There is one body and one Spirit—
just as you were called to one hope when you were called--
one Lord, one faith, one baptism;
one God and Father of all,
who is over all and through all and in all."*
Ephesians 4:4-6 (NIV)

Outline of Ephesians Chapter 4

1-3	Unity of the believers in the Spirit of God
4-6	The seven-fold unity of the church
7-10	The ascended Lord gives gifts of grace to His Church
11-16	The office and ministry and its function
17-19	Putting away the sins of the Gentiles
20-24	Putting on the New Man
25-32	Various Christian Virtues—Second Table of the law (lying, being angry, stealing, evil spirit, kindness, forgiving)

The first three chapters of Ephesians lay a doctrinal foundation, as taught by Paul. The next three chapters build off this doctrine into a practical description of ways to glorify God within the Church.

    1. Can there be diversity in unity? Explain.

Sometimes Christians get "unity" and "unison" mixed up. Unison means to do things the same way at the same time. In music, to sing in unison means that everyone sings the same notes at the same time. Unity might better be compared to harmony. When we sing in harmony we are all in the same key, but we sing different notes at different times. When all of these actions are joined together we see and hear a beautiful sound. Unity does not mean being identical; rather, different actions blending in harmony for the same purpose.

Read Ephesians 4:1-16

    2. Paul is openly concerned for these Christians, so much so that he begs them to live a life "worthy of their calling." Remembering what we read in the first three chapters, what is this calling?

 *PONDER THIS: What is your calling? Is it different from that of the Ephesians? Is anyone challenging you to live up to your calling?*

3. List the characteristics of life that reflect our calling. (v. 1-3)

4. Who does this list of characteristics remind you of?

5. List four characteristics from your list in question 3 in the table below and give examples of others in Scripture that demonstrated that characteristic. The first row is filled in as an example.

Humility	Daniel

6. Why are these characteristics so important in the life of a believer in light of Galatians 5:22-23?

PONDER THIS: Which of these characteristics is most evident in your life? Why do you think that is true? Which is most lacking? How might you improve this?

7. What are the seven marks of the Church found in Ephesians 4?

8. How do these marks make us (the Church) a unique people?

9. Who is the giver of the gifts? (v. 7)

10. Why is verse 7 such an important statement?

11. Read verse 8 along with Psalm 68:18. What is different? What is the same?

Verse 8 is a free verse quotation of Psalm 68:18. This is applied to Christ as "Christus Victor" or Christ the Victor. The change in wording is most likely due to the rabbinic interpretations current in Paul's day that read the Hebrew preposition "from" in the sense of "to" (a meaning it often has), and the verb for "received" in the sense of "take and give" (a meaning it sometimes has). Thus "received from" is translated and understood as "take and give to." Paul is not considered incorrect in his use of this Psalm because "All Scripture is God-breathed!"

Prayer

Lord, we thank you for the blessing of reading your Word together. We ask that these words of life, truth, and hope would continue to impact us in the week ahead. Help us seek unity around the truth of your Word in our relationships and our churches. May your love and grace follow each of us as we return to our daily lives, refreshed and blessed by you.

For Next Week

As you prepare for next week, read through the entire book of Ephesians. Then make a list of reasons to be thankful for your local church, the body of Christ. Also, consider a verse from chapter one that stands out to you most, and why you think that was.

Memory Challenge

[4] There is one body and one Spirit—just as you were called to one hope when you were called— [5] one Lord, one faith, one baptism; [6] one God and Father of all, who is over all and through all and in all.
Ephesians 4:4-6 (NIV)

EIGHT

Ephesians 4:11-32
A New Way of Thinking

"So I tell you this, and insist on it in the Lord, that you must no longer live as the Gentiles do, in the futility of their thinking."
Ephesians 4:17

1. For what reason were the gifts listed in verse 11 given? (v. 12-16)

 **PONDER THIS:** *What gift do you recognize in yourself that builds up the body of Christ?*

Read Ephesians 4:17-32.

2. How does Paul describe the life of the Gentile/unbeliever? (**Note:** *this way of life was theirs by choice. They gave themselves up to it.*)

3. What are some examples of this thinking in our world today?

PONDER THIS: What are some ways you find yourself slipping into this way of thinking?

4. Read verses 25-32 and list what we are to "put off" and what we are to "put on."

5. What is our reason for this change?

 PONDER THIS: *As you reflect on the previous Ponder This question, what are some intentional ways you can be made new in the attitude of your mind and put on the new self?*

6. What will help us to "forgive one another, as God has forgiven you"?

7. "The church is the only institution on the planet that exists for the benefit of those that are not yet her members" (author unknown). Do you agree or disagree with this statement? Why?

8. If applied to your congregation, how does that statement affect the mission of your congregation?

Prayer

Good Father, thank you for all the things you have done today. Thank you for your love that you have revealed to us through your Word. We pray over all the words that you have sown into our hearts today. Watch over them, protect them, and help them take root in our lives. And as we leave this place now, thank you that you walk with us. For yours is the kingdom, the power, and the glory both in this age, and in the age to come.

For Next Week

As you prepare for next week, read through chapters 5 and 6, which close out Paul's letter to the Ephesians. Consider how these chapters are the perfect ending to this powerful Epistle.

Memory Challenge

[32] *Be kind to one another, tenderhearted, forgiving one another, as God in Christ forgave you.*
Ephesians 4:32 (ESV)

NINE

Ephesians 5:1-21
The Marriage Chapter

*"Be very careful, then, how you live—
not as unwise but as wise,
making the most of every opportunity,
because the days are evil."*
Ephesians 5:15-16

Outline of Ephesians Chapter 5

1-2   Admonition to brotherly love

3-7   Admonition to purity of living

8-18   The life of witnessing to the Word (so as to influence the world for Christ)

19-21   Admonition to comfort and edify each other through the singing of hymns to the Lord (Worship and the Church)

22-24   Table of Duties: Admonition to Christian wives

25-30   Table of Duties: Admonition to Christian husbands

31-33   The institution of marriage and final admonition to husbands and to wives

"Be imitators of God, therefore, as dearly loved children..." These words of Paul to the Ephesians set the tone for the section we will look at in today's study. Paul is simply arguing that children are like their parents, a fact that can be both encouraging and embarrassing to those of us who have children. Have you ever seen a child playing "house" or dressing up in their mother or father's oversized clothes? Or zig-zagging the lawn with their plastic bubble mowers? These types of imitation are heart-warming. Of course, on the other hand, children will also learn inappropriate behavior and language if that's the parental example set in their home. You've probably heard the saying, "Do as I say, not as I do." Children probably learn more by watching and imitating than any other way.

If we hold to our wonderful claim as "Children of God," then we ought to imitate our Father. This is the basis for the three admonitions in this section. God is love (1 John 4:8); therefore, walk in love (v. 1-2). God is light (1 John 1:5); therefore, walk as children of light (v. 8). God is truth (1 John 5:6); therefore, walk in wisdom (v. 15-17).

Read Ephesians 4:32–5:21.

1. What are a few things you have observed about God which you have begun, or could begin, to imitate? (Some of these observations come from watching God work through others; some might come from watching God work in Scripture.)

2. What kind of love is Paul talking about (v. 1-2)? What are some words to describe this love?

3. How is Christ the perfect example of what Paul asks of us? (v. 2)

 ***Ponder This: Trivia that is far from trivial...***

Through all of Scripture, wherever a listing of "sins" or causes of sin is found, sexual sins always are always at the head of the list. Why might that be?

4. How is thanksgiving an appropriate replacement for the behavior Paul condemns in 5:3-4?

5. Why will immoral, impure, or greedy people be unable to inherit the Kingdom? (v. 5-7)

6. Why are such people considered idolaters?

7. Is there help for idolaters? (See 1 Cor. 6:9-11)

LUTHER SPEAKS

> "Not only the adoration of images is idolatry, but also trust in one's own righteousness, works and merits, and putting confidence in riches and power. As the latter is the commonest, so it also is the most noxious."
>
> (from *What Luther Said*)

 ***Ponder This:*** *The harsh reality is that there is a little idolatry in all of our lives. What form of idolatry do you most struggle with in your life?*

8. Where in our culture do we see modern-day idolatry? What role do we play in contributing to this, or detracting from this cultural idolatry?

9. In verses 8-14, Paul contrasts light and darkness to say more about holy living. According to these verses, what does it mean to "live as children of the light"?

10. Often we equate wisdom with intelligence. What characterizes wise people, according to Paul? (v. 15-17)

> ***Ponder This:*** *The English NIV in verse 18 reads, "Instead, be filled <u>with the spirit</u>." In the original Greek it best reads to be "be filled <u>in Spirit</u>" speaking of an indwelling of the Spirit, not just working with. How might these two understandings look differently in your life (cooperation <u>with the Spirit</u> vs. living <u>in Spirit</u>)?*

11. Verses 19-21 look like four separate commands in English. In Greek, however, they are linked grammatically to verse 18 and describe several beneficial results of being filled with the Spirit. In your own words, explain the characteristics of those who are filled with the Spirit.

A lot of emotion and misunderstanding surrounds the word "submit" and the words of this text. So, try to come to this text as if you had never seen it before. Try to set aside your own biases and see what Paul has said on the subject of submission.

While most modern translations separate verses 1-17 from verses 21-33, there is no clear separation—either in the grammar or in the thoughts of Paul.

Read Ephesians 5:21-33.

12. How does verse 21 both preview this section and tie this section in with the first part of chapter five?

13. How is the responsibility of headship pointed out in a) verses 24-25 and b) verses 26-27?

14. The concept that is often missunderstood when these verses are viewed is the fact that "Headship ≠ Domination." How does this concept relate to us as children of God?

15. In verse 31, Paul quotes Genesis 2:24 to root his arguments about the unity of husband and wife in creation itself. How do verses 31-33 summarize his teaching on the unity that is to exist between wives and husbands?

16. How does chapter five fit in to Ephesians as "The Church, the Body of Christ"?

Prayer

Lord help us to clothe ourselves in the image and knowledge of Christ. Remind us of our newness in you, and the amazing power given to us for this change. Help us to encourage and challenge the whole body of Christ to live in you, and fill our hearts and lips with words of gratitude. Amen.

For Next Week

As you prepare for the last week of our study, read through the entire book of Ephesians. This will help refresh all the themes of this book, and prepare you to discuss its concluding chapter.

Memory Challenge

[1] Therefore be imitators of God, as beloved children. [2] And walk in love, as Christ loved us and gave himself up for us, a fragrant offering and sacrifice to God.
Ephesians 5:1-2 (ESV)

TEN

Ephesians 6
Children, Parents, Slaves, Masters

*"Children, obey your parents in the Lord,
for this is right."*
Ephesians 6:1 (NIV)

Outline of Ephesians Chapter 6

1-3	Table of Duties: Duties of children to parents
4	Table of Duties: Admonition to fathers
5-8	Table of Duties: Admonition to slaves
9	Table of Duties: Admonition to slave owners
10-17	The "Panoply of God" (the armor of the Lord)
18-20	The role of prayer in the battle of faith
21-24	Conclusion – Final Greetings

After watching a television presentation about rebellious youth, a husband said to his wife, "What a mess! Where did our generation go wrong?" The wife calmly replied, "We had children!"

It seems no matter where we look in modern society, we see antagonism, division, and rebellion. Husbands and wives are divorcing each other; children are rebelling against their parents; and employers and employees are seeking new ways to avoid strikes and keep the machinery of industry running productively. We have tried education, legislation, and every other approach, but nothing seems to work. Paul's solution to the antagonism both in the home and in society was regeneration—a new heart from God and a new level of submission to Christ and to one another. God's greatest program is "to bring all things on heaven and on earth together under one head" (Ephesians 1:10). Paul indicates that this spiritual harmony begins in the lives of Christians who are submitted to the Lordship of Christ.

Read Ephesians 6:1-9.

1. How do these passages continue the theme of mutual submission begun in 5:21?

2. What reasons are given for honoring and obeying parents? (v. 1-3)

LUTHER SPEAKS

> *"If God's Word and will are placed first and observed, nothing ought to be considered more important than the will and word of our parents, provided that these, too, are subordinated to obedience toward God and are not set into opposition to the preceding commandments.*
>
> *...In addition, it would be well to preach to parents on the nature of their office, how they should treat those committed to their authority.*
>
> *...Parents should consider that they owe obedience to God, and that above all, they should earnestly and faithfully discharge the duties of their office, not only to provide for the material support of their children, servants, subjects, etc., but especially to bring them up to the praise and honor of God."*
>
> (from *Luther's Large Catechism*)

3. How can fathers and mothers exasperate their children? (v.4)

4. Why does Paul contrast exasperating children with bringing "them up in the training and instruction of the Lord"? (v. 4)

5. What is implied about the way bondservants typically worked for their masters? (v. 5-8)

6. How and why were Christian slaves to be different?

7. What implications does this have for how employers treat employees?

Prayer Wars

In a war of bullets, careful aim and heavy armor win battles. In a war of words, eloquent speech and sharp pens overcome the opposition. But if the fight is outside the realm of sight, sound, and tongue, how are victories won? Let's take a look at Paul's answers as we focus on the close of Ephesians.

Read Ephesians 6:10-20.

8. Paul emphasizes that our struggle is not with flesh and blood. How has he emphasized this same point elsewhere in his letter?

When Paul wrote Ephesians, he may have been chained to a Roman soldier (6:20). Whether chained to or guarded by a Roman soldier, Paul no doubt had more experience than he wanted with soldiers. This could easily have inspired his analogy of 6:13-17.

9. List the pieces of armor, how Paul describes them, and their purpose as listed by Paul.

Protection	Description	Function
belt	Belt of truth	Help us know truth from error.

10. Paul mentions twice (v. 11 & 13) to put on the whole armor of God. Why does he emphasize the whole armor?

11. Having been fitted with the Armor of God, what steps does Paul mention to empower us to stand?

Ponder This: *How many battles are won by standing still? Yet that is exactly what God calls us to do. What's different about this battle?*

12. In 6:18-20, Paul urges all kinds of prayers. How has he been a model prayer warrior throughout this letter?

13. What main obstacle do you face in fighting the battle of prayer more effectively?

 **Ponder This:** *How intentional does a soldier need to be in preparing for battle? How intentional are you in "dressing" for battle each day? How could you make this preparation a more intentional part of your day?*

Prayer

Lord, you call us your chosen people, holy and dearly loved. Help us to reflect who you see in us to those in our family and at our job. We rejoice that you are over us and in us as we live this new life. Help us to live a life that demands an explanation. Grant us words to share the story of your Lordship in our lives. Lord Jesus, help us to know you more and more each day. Amen.

Memory Challenge

[10] *Finally, be strong in the Lord and in the strength of his might.* [11] *Put on the whole armor of God, that you may be able to stand against the schemes of the devil.*
Ephesians 6:10-11

Final Thought…..

Read Ephesians 6:21-24.

Paul from prison writes to encourage the church. But even the letter is not enough for Paul, so he sends Tychicus [TIKE ih kuhs] with the letter, to assure the saints about Paul's welfare.

Tychicus was a Christian from the province of Asia (see Acts 20:4). He was a faithful friend, fellow worker, and messenger of the Apostle Paul. With other disciples, he traveled ahead of Paul from Macedonia to Troas, where he waited for Paul's arrival.

BIBLE STUDY LEADER'S GUIDE

*"All Scripture is God-breathed
and is useful for teaching, rebuking,
correcting and training in righteousness,
so that the man of God
may be thoroughly equipped for every good work."*
2 Timothy 3:16-17 (NIV)

TIPS FOR LEADERS

PREPARATION
Prayer is the best way to start your preparation each week. Next, make sure you have taken the time to work through the study yourself, reading through any leader's notes provided. Make notes of your thoughts in your study guide as you prepare. Make note of any additional text you wish to use that is not listed in the material.

Without preparation, it can be easy to give too much time to the early questions in the study, which doesn't leave enough time to work through all that you hoped to cover. In your preparation, mark the key questions and topics you want to make sure to cover.

BEGIN ON TIME
One of our greatest issues when leading a Bible study is time. It is a finite resource, and your students have committed to a set starting and ending time. While it is important to allow students to greet each other and catch up on their personal lives, try to allow

"pre-study time" for this (i.e., meet at 6:30 with the study beginning at 7:00 and ending at 8:00).

When the study does not start when promised, two things happen. The first is very simple: you run the risk of running out of time to complete the lesson. The second is the snowball effect—when students know you don't start on time, so they don't show up on time. This issue snowballs until those who are good about getting there on time stop coming out of sheer frustration.

If you establish a culture of starting on time, regardless of whether or not everyone in the group has arrived, and not allowing latecomers to interrupt your discussion when they arrive, you will find that group members become more punctual.

END ON TIME
Okay, so you probably know where this one is going. Just as critical to getting a good start is wrapping up in a timely fashion. If you do not honor the time commitments that the group has agreed to, it becomes a source of frustration. When this happens, students leave class not remembering the lesson of the day, but remembering how they felt about class running over.

PRAYER REQUESTS
There is something meaningful in a small group sharing life together by taking time to include the sharing of prayer requests. However, we also know that sometimes sharing requests can easily turn into story time as people want to fill in back story on their requests. This in turn often opens the door for lengthy discussions as other members offer advice or input.

There are two ways you can deal with this issue. The first is to simple figure in time to allow for this conversation. This might mean ending the study time 15 minutes early to allow for the prayer requests. A better way perhaps might be to provide note cards for people to write down their requests and share them at the end or simply have members swap cards with someone else.

THE MAIN THING

It can be a lot of work to keep the main thing, the main thing. In this case, the main thing is The Word. There are any number of reasons why people choose to attend a particular Bible study. They also come with varying biblical background and interest. It can be easy for your group to slip from being a Bible study group into becoming more of a personal support group. Trying to find that right balance between biblical study and personal support is a significant challenge for every small-group leader.

As group members become more comfortable with one another, they become more comfortable in what they share with the group. Times may even arise when, due to a personal need of a member, the idea of setting aside the study to use that time to listen, advise, and encourage might become an issue. While there may be extenuating circumstances, you should be extremely cautious about using your regular time for this.

God has promised that His word is living and active. The Word of God speaks into every need and situation in our lives. It heals, it gives perspective, it instructs, convicts, restores, and renews. Please do not assume that the advice and discussion of the group has more power than your discussion of the truths of God's Word to help that hurting person.

IS THAT COFFEE I SMELL?

There is nothing like a cup of coffee and a few goodies to help a study move along. I am a firm believer in a little food fellowship with Bible study. I have yet to be in a small group study where someone does not have a desire to help provide or arrange for goodies. Don't let this tip seem trite as compared to the rest—and if it does, think it over again with a cup of coffee and a Danish!

SUGGESTED ANSWERS TO THE STUDY QUESTIONS

Lesson One

1) They were believers, but perhaps did not fully realize what that meant.
2) He is an Apostle of Christ—he declares his authority to his readers.
3) Saints equate them with believers. Paul further defines that as "faithful in Christ Jesus."
4) Answers may vary.
5) The grace and peace extended comes not from Paul but through Paul from God the Father and Christ.
6) (v. 4) He – Father, him – Son, him – Father, (v. 5) he – Father, his – Father, (v6) his – Father, he – Father, he – Father, (v. 7) him – Son, his – Christ, (v. 8) he – Father, (v. 9) he – Father, his – Father, his – Father, he – Father, *[list drawn from NIV text]*
7) It was the Father's plan before the foundation of the world through the Son.
8) The Trinity shares a unique closeness and unity working together. "Anyone who has seen me has seen the Father," (John 14:9).
9) We were bought out of the slavery of sin through the blood of Jesus.
10) "The first to hope in Christ," the Jews who acknowledged to the Messiah (v. 13). "You also were included in Christ," the Gentiles who heard and believed the truth of Jesus. Both are now as one in Christ to the praise of His glory.
11) Baptism is the seal. In the baptism service, the child receives "the sign of the Cross both upon the forehead and upon the heart to mark you as one redeemed by Christ the crucified."

Lesson Two

1) Answers may vary. (Paul prays more of a rushing mountain stream)
2) Needs of people, health, family, relationship, safety...
3) Their love and faith in Christ, coupled with their love for the saints.
4) They fulfilled the "great commandment"—Love the Lord your God with all your heart, soul, mind, and strength, and love your neighbor as your self. This covers both the first and second table of the Law.
5) The hope to which they were called; the riches of His glorious inheritance; immeasurable greatness of His power (salvation) to all who believe.
6) He prays and celebrates their faith in Jesus Christ, as he prays for their faith in Jesus Christ.

Lesson Three

1) Sin separates us from the Father. "The wages of sin is death" (Romans 6:23).
2) I would be toast; we might not have been born, the world would be in total chaos; we would live in fear because of our actions.
3) Because of His great love for us. "Being rich in mercy" "even when we were dead."
4) We have done nothing to merit God's love or mercy; we were not giving Him any honor or respect; "we were enemies of God" (Romans 5:10).
5) The will of God—not based on our doing but on God's will. Even Paul operates under the will of God.
6) No, these are two different things: verses 8-9 are talking about justification, and verse 10 is talking about sanctification.
7) Proclaim the good news; obedience to His Word; make disciples.

Lesson Four

1) They were without hope; outside of the covenants; separated from God.
2) Name-calling; uncircumcised.
3) Answers may vary.
4) Covenants (multiple; v. 12); Not from Israel; Temple was a barrier—Gentiles could not approach God in the Temple (v. 14).
5) Brought close through the blood of Christ; members of God's household; no longer strangers.
6) Through Christ, barriers are broken and removed; reconciled through the cross; the tearing of the Temple curtain.
7) Both Israel and the Gentiles had to change their thinking; Israel no longer viewed God as contained in the Temple and exclusive to them as a nation. The Gentiles had to recognize that there is but one God, not community, or national gods.
8) Members of one household; one community; fellow citizens in Christ; becoming one holy temple; the Church is the people, not the building.
9) Christ is the cornerstone of both the Old Testament and the New Testament.
10) It is open to all who believe and place their trust in Jesus Christ as Lord and Savior.

Lesson Five

1) Answers may vary.
2) Mystery made know to me by revelation (v. 3); made a servant or minister (v.7); to preach to the Gentiles (v. 8).
3) The Gentiles are fellow heirs; members of the body of Christ; share in the promise of Christ.
4) Paul who once thought of the Gentiles as the lowest, now calls himself the least of all God's people (and the

mystery is now open to the least). The mystery also becomes the driving force for his preaching, his confidence and his purpose.
5) Paul thought salvation was only for the Children of Israel—this was a radical thought for the Jews.
6) Make known the Wisdom of God. To the rulers and authorities in the heavenly places; these are the evil powers that seek to destroy God's people; we (the Church) announce unity among all God's people, giving them no room to rule or invade. Christ has triumphed over them all.
7) The overall purpose is to unite the Church as one body through Christ—who is the head of the Church.
8) So that they don't lose heart or grow discouraged.

Lesson Six

1) Paul kneels to pray. He takes a posture of respect and humility before His Father.
2) Strengthened in power through the Spirit (v. 16); Christ may dwell in your hearts (v. 17); Grasp the size of God's love (v. 18); Know that love beyond reason.
3) The vastness of God's love for them.
4) It was hard because a) we don't know how to love perfectly; b) they were living under persecution—even Paul was in prison.
5) We often run through a list of needs, for healing, for physical needs. We pray for the urgent, and not always the important.
6) Answers may vary.
7) The power is in Christ—through His body the Church, not our power. God's eternal power (see Ephesians 1:20).
8) Because God can do more than we ask or imagine.

Lesson Seven

1) Yes. Answers may vary.
2) To do good works, while living and working in unity with the Gentile believers—who also live by grace through faith in Christ.
3) Humility, gentleness, patience, love, unity, peace.
4) It reminds us of Jesus, who showed us this perfectly.
5) Answers will vary.
6) They are the fruit of the Spirit in believers. These are not options, or something that only some people get—these ARE the fruit of the Spirit in us. They are our lived-out calling.
7) One body, one spirit; one hope; one Lord; one faith; one baptism; one God & Father of all.
8) We have unity on so many levels in a world where we can't seem to find unity on any level, not to mention 7 levels. In Scripture, the number 7 is also seen as a mark of completeness—we are complete in our unity.
9) Christ.
10) This grace was given to each one of us.
11) In Psalm 68 he receives gifts from men; in verse 8 he gives gifts to men.

Lesson Eight

1) To prepare (equip) God's people for their calling.
2) Listing may include the following depending on translation: futile thinking, darkened thinking, aliens, sensual, greedy, corrupt, deceitful, callous, lust, impurity.
3) Answers may vary.
4) Put off: lies; in anger don't sin; stealing; negative talk; corrupting talk, bitterness, wrath, anger, slander, malice. Put on: honesty, in anger stop and think, encouragement, kind compassion, forgiving.
5) Sealed by the Holy Spirit (v. 19). Forgiven by Christ (v. 32).

6) Answers may vary.
7) Answers may vary.
8) We think less of our selves (less elitism) and more about others (more like a rescue mission).

Lesson Nine

1) Forgiveness; patient; loves even his enemies (some of these observations come from watching God work through others, some might come from watching God work in Scripture).
2) *Agape* love—Unconditional, sacrificial, perfect, complete (1 John 3:1).
3) He is love (1 John 4:8, 16—God is love). He is an offering and sacrifice.
4) Takes our eyes off of ourselves and the world & focuses on God and His blessings.
5) They are idolaters—they do not trust in God.
6) They place other things or desires before God.
7) We can be washed clean, sanctified, and justified in the name of Jesus Christ by the Spirit of God.
8) Professional sports team allegiance, political parties, homes, cars, jobs...
9) Avoid it—have nothing to do with it; Expose it—shine like on the darkness to make it visible; Share it—what is good, right, and true.
10) Making the most of opportunities and understanding the Lord's will.
11) This is not a command, but a reflection of a life filled with the Spirit: speak to each other with Scripture and song, they are grateful people who willingly submit and serve one another.
12) The submission spoken of in verse 22 is like the reflection of the Spirit we see in verse 21. This submission is seen in Christ as He submits to the Father. "Be imitators of God."

13) A) The husband is called to lay down his life for the sake of his bride. B) He is to defend her honor and her view by the world.
14) God has given us free will and does not force His control over us; therefore, we are not called to live in domination over one another.
15) Part of the basic (Genesis) plan for the earth. Like the relationship Christ has with His Church—a very close relationship.
16) Chapter five is the practical "how to live as the body of Christ" portion of the letter.

Lesson Ten

1) The circle widens to include children, parents, bondservants, and masters.
2) That things will go your way and you will have a long life.
3) Answers may vary.
4) We do not just "train" them by saying, "because I said so," but by teaching, "because this is what God wants and why."
5) They were more obedient when being watched, and they served grudgingly.
6) Whole-heartedly, respectfully, sincerely; they are to seem as if they were serving Christ Himself.
7) They are to treat them with respect, sincerity, without threat, as a brother.
8) Prince of the power of the air, raised to Heavenly Places (2:2-6). Darkness and light (5:8-11).
9) Answers may vary.
10) If we leave something off we become vulnerable.
11) Prayer—at all times in the Spirit.
12) He speaks of prayer (1:16); He models prayer (3:14-21); He invites prayers (6:19-20).
13) Answers may vary.

ABOUT THE AUTHOR

Craig McCourt is a gifted storyteller, author, speaker, and pastor. For 30 years, Craig McCourt ministered full-time to youth and their families, using his remarkable teaching style to present biblical truths in ways that motivate change in believers' lives.

Craig currently serves as Pastor of Peace Lutheran Church in Arlington, Minnesota. For more on Peace Lutheran Church visit www.peacearlington.org. This is Craig's second experience as Lead Pastor and he greatly enjoys the opportunity to preach and teach using the stories of Scripture he loves.

Craig's first book, *Pondering God—Seeing God in Everyday Life*, is a 30-day devotional and is available through his website or from Amazon and Barnes & Noble. He also hosts a video podcast called *Pondering God: with Craig McCourt*. You can subscribe to his videos as well as listen online to current and classic episodes of the PonderingGod podcast by visiting www.CraigMcCourt.com.

Over the years, Craig has been blessed to speak to hundreds of groups, both large and small. He has had the opportunity to speak internationally, as well as in many different places across the United States. Shirley, Craig's wife of more than 30 years, joins him as the PonderingGod ministry grows. Shirley brings many years of camp and retreat experience to PonderingGod, as well as a heart for ministering to women.

The mission of PonderingGod is:
As disciples of Christ, we seek to use the stories of Scripture and life to proclaim the works of God and ponder what He has done, encouraging and equipping others to do the same.

For more on their ministry, visit **www.ponderinggod.org**

The Body of Christ Is Called to Serve
World Servants Mission Trips:
Everyone Is Welcome

My wife and I have partnered with World Servants for many years. We invite you to discover the joy and power of serving on a World Servants mission trip.

By going on a World Servants mission trip, you can make a difference by strengthening families, engaging congregations, bringing hope to communities, and giving God an opportunity to touch the lives of many.

World Servants' mission is to mobilize a global network of people to impact the world through Jesus Christ by responding to physical and spiritual needs—and to develop and facilitate life-changing learning and serving experiences that bring hope to the world.

A World Servants short-term mission is a week-long experience for groups, families, and individuals to assist in what God is doing in a specific community. The foundation of our ministry is to enter every relationship and experience with the attitude of a Learner, Servant and Storyteller. We hold to the value of learning about the community in which we serving, coming alongside those God is working through, and demonstrating care and concern in a way that preserves dignity.

The mission is to meet both the physical and spiritual needs of our "neighbors" through acts of service, i.e. construction, rebuilding projects, painting tasks, and yard upkeep, as well as ministry outreach activities such as Kids' Club, Sports Camp, women's ministry, home visits, community worship and gatherings.

Trip participant needs are taken care of as World Servants provides food, housing, transportation, construction and ministry materials, t-shirt, journal and World Servants trip facilitators who have long-term relationships with community leaders. Each evening a World Servants mission leader will guide the group through a reflection process, while challenging the group to continue a life of service.

All our mission experiences are designed to have a long-term impact. Families value experiences which incorporate the whole family, to be a part of a physical experience of hands-on, face to face interactions with people where their presence and service makes a difference that is directly felt, seen and heard. A comment often heard is, *"This was a defining moment in my life and in the life of our family. We will never be the same."*

To learn about World Servants' life-changing mission trips, please visit our website: ***www.worldservants.org***

Other products from PonderingGod

Pondering God
Looking for a little inspiration for the day? Want a devotional to start your next church meeting? This book may be just what you are looking for. *Pondering God* is a collection of stories, sometimes humorous, always designed to help you see God in everyday life. These stories are filled with Scripture and each contain a question designed to get you Pondering God.

My Heart Christ's Home – Retreat Kit
This retreat kit, which could also be used as a series of 6-8 Bible studies, tries to get at some of these deeper meanings of Ephesians 3:16-17. If Christ dwells in us, that means that our bodies are His home. He lives here. By taking a look at different rooms in this "home" we begin to understand more fully how these verses impact our lives. This retreat package includes everything you need for your Bible Study portion of a Women's Retreat and includes some ideas for games, quiet times, music, and other program areas of your retreat.

Knowing Christ – Small Group Study
Do you desire to know Christ more, and lead others to know Him too? You are not alone. Many of Paul's prayers for the early church are found in his letters. The theme of his prayer is always centered around his call for them to "Know Christ." He prays that they would know the depth of Christ's love, the power of His wisdom, the sufficiency of His grace, and continue to grow in their knowledge of Him. In this 9-week small group study we walk verse by verse through Paul's letter to the Colossian Church.

WHAT OTHERS SAY

Craig's unique ability to bring God's word into how we live our lives and make it so easy to apply has truly encouraged me. He is not shy about sharing his own faith journey and that makes his messages that much more real and inspiring.
Rick, Retreat Participant

If you are looking for a Christian speaker, teacher or a leader for a retreat, Craig is the one to hire! His natural caring spirit and ability to break down God's Word is refreshing and engaging for the listener. Craig's humble spirit pours out onto you and you can't help but want what Craig has!
Jana, Event Participant

Craig's teaching is engaging for young and old alike. He has a unique ability to teach God's word in a way that is down to earth, clear and relevant for today. His sense of humor brings lots of laughter and fun, making the time spent enjoyable and memorable.
Jason, Bible Class Participant

"This guy is a funny, funny man"
Rev. Dr. Jeffery Schrank – Christ Church Lutheran
- Pheonix AZ

"I have seen God use Craig through engaging his audience by bringing God's Word to meet them where they are at BUT no one leaves without their lives transformed by the power of the Holy Spirit."
Traci Kohls - Adjunct Faculty at
Concordia University St. Paul

"Craig McCourt is one of the most inspiring, yet down-to-earth speakers I have ever had the opportunity to listen to. His God-given talents are many. I particularly like the fact that Craig is extremely effective in motivating and uplifting people of all age groups--teens, parents, seniors--with his love for the Lord."
Dr. James Pingel - Secondary Education Department Chair -
Concordia University Wisconsin

www.ingramcontent.com/pod-product-compliance
Lightning Source LLC
Chambersburg PA
CBHW071728040426
42446CB00011B/2268